The Offic

Part of the royalties f
donated to The Ashton
second Sunday in Octo
Championships in Ash ... pshire and all
proceeds are donated to charities for the blind.

THE OFFICIAL CONKER BOOK

JEFF CLOVES

Illustrated by
KEN MAHOOD

JONATHAN CAPE
LONDON

First published 1993
© Jeff Cloves
© Illustrations Ken Mahood

JONATHAN CAPE
20 Vauxhall Bridge Road, London SW1V 2SA

Jeff Cloves has asserted his right to be
identified as the author of this work.

A CIP catalogue record for this book
is available from the British Library

ISBN 0-224-03538-x

Filmset by SX Composing Ltd, Rayleigh, Essex
Printed and bound by
Cox and Wyman Ltd, Reading

ACKNOWLEDGEMENTS

My love and gratitude to my mum and dad for giving me a childhood in that town of horse chestnut tree-lined streets, Cheltenham Spa, and my thanks to the following for their help and assistance:

Ashton Conker Club, Common Ground, Pete Frame, Heather Godwin (whose idea this book is), Benny Green, John Hadman, Richard Mabey, Sean Magee, Mike Milne, Iona Opie, John and Sylvià Sena, Dominique Shead.

The section on playing conkers in *Children's Games in Street and Playground* by Iona and Peter Opie (Oxford University Press 1969) was an invaluable source.

The extract from *How to be topp* by Willans and Searle is reprinted by permission of Pavilion Books and the extracts from *Poisonous plants and fungi* and *Poisonous plants in Britain* by permission of H.M.S.O.

Going conkering

If you are nine or twelve years old or
ten or six or eight
conkering is a passing craze but
let me put you straight:
when yellow chestnut leaves are lying on
October's cooling ground
and a spiky shell splits open to
reveal the rich red-brown
of the seed inside the green case gleaming
so seductively
that you slip it in your pocket as you
scuff home to your tea
four hundred years ago remember
boys and girls – a lot like you
were kicking up the leaves to find that
gleaming conker too.

LIST OF CONTENTS

CHAPTER ONE

HOW IT ALL BEGAN

Common conkers

Conker trees are everywhere. You may not have one in your garden but next door might have and is that the crown of one just visible over those distant roofs? Perhaps they line your street or adorn the public garden in the square. I bet there are some in your nearest park or round the boundaries of the local cricket ground. They are the tallest and stateliest of our ornamental trees, but now you will probably see more of them in the town than in the country. Even so, there may be one in your school playground, whether you go to an inner city modern that's all glass and concrete or a village traditional with red and yellow brickwork and churchy windows.

Prehistoric conkers

The European horse chestnut is a distant ancestor of trees that now grow in the mountains of the USA and eastern Asia. Fossil evidence tells us that about a million years ago a belt of warm-climate forest circled the northern hemisphere. The trees would have been large and exotic and the huge compound leaves of the horse chestnut and its enormous seeds or conkers, give just a hint of that warm primeval world.

'Great-rooted blossomer'

The common horse chestnut is the tallest and finest of the chestnuts and it can grow to over 30m in height, and spread 15m from its trunk. The older trees often have a twist in the trunk and the tree is a fast grower reaching 12m in twenty years. Because it grows so quickly, the wood is soft and although the diameter of the trunk can reach 2m, it is not hard enough to use for large pieces of furniture. Sometimes it is used for small items like wooden toys, handles on kitchen utensils and brushes, fruit storage trays and for making the shapes and patterns for objects which are then manufactured in metal. Sometimes furniture makers use it to decorate cupboards and chairs made from harder wood. The horse chestnut is not a woodland tree,

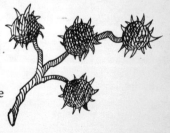

although self-seeded trees can be found on the fringes of woods. It is more commonly found growing singly or in groves and avenues to provide shade and beauty. It is early to leaf and early to drop and at my junior school we used to keep jam jars of conker sticky buds which would burst into leaf after they were picked.

Foreign conkers

The conker tree or horse chestnut – fancy name, *aesculus hippocastanum* – is one of our most loved trees. It grows throughout the British Isles, though it is still more numerous in the south of England and for a long time was thought to be a native tree. Its true home is in the mountainous regions of Greece, Albania, Bulgaria and Turkey. European visitors found Turks feeding conkers to sick horses as medicine – and seeds (conkers) from Constantinople (now Istanbul) were planted in Vienna in 1576. Thereafter the spread in popularity of the horse chestnut was rapid.

How it all began

English conkers

The precise date of the conker's arrival in England is not known but we do know that the great English gardener, John Tradescant (1570-1638), who travelled widely in Europe, successfully grew a conker tree in his garden in Lambeth. Whatever, it is widely thought that the tree was established in England during the reign of Elizabeth I (1558-1603) and that European settlers took it to America too.

Travelling conkers

Here's a theory. The spread of the horse chestnut tree across Europe is curiously similar to the spread or *diaspora* of Gypsies from their original homeland in central India. The first record of Gypsies in England is 1514. The earliest suggested arrival of the conker is 1557 but could it be that it was brought here by Gypsies – and much earlier than supposed?

Horse shoes and horse chestnuts

The Gypsies' own language, Romani, has been enlarged by words borrowed from the countries they settled in or passed through. There are words of Greek and Persian origin in Romani and in India Gypsies were known as metal workers or smiths. The Romani word *petulengro*

means smith and comes from the word *petalo* which means horse shoe in both Romani and Greek. Smith is a very common Gypsy surname and it is not surprising that horse-drawn travellers should be their own blacksmiths and also sell that service to others. What is true (see *Conquers all known ills* page 59) is that Gypsies used conkers as medicine and food and would have carried them on their travels. The link between the village blacksmith standing under the spreading chestnut tree and the flashy dark-skinned immigrants may have at least as much to it as meets the eye.

Under the spreading chestnut tree

When they were at school, my mum and dad learned by heart a poem by the American poet, Henry Wadsworth Longfellow, called 'The Village Blacksmith'. Your grandparents probably learned it too. It was an incredibly popular poem written in 1862. Here are the opening lines:

> *Under a spreading chestnut tree*
> *The village smithy stands;*
> *The smith a mighty man is he,*
> *With large and sinewy hands;*
> *And the muscles on his brawny arms,*
> *Are strong as iron bands.*

From then on blacksmiths were always associated with horse chestnuts and the tree is still invariably described as 'spreading'. Longfellow lived in Cambridge, Massachusetts and on his 72nd birthday school children presented him with a chair made from the very tree under which the blacksmith stood. Who knows, perhaps Longfellow's blacksmith really was a descendant of one of those travelling Gypsy blacksmiths who always had a conker in his pocket.

A chestnut grazing on chestnuts

What's in a name?

The usual explanation given for the name horse chestnut is the old story of the Turks feeding conkers to sick horses. Then there is the leaf scar left when the leaves fall. It is shaped like a horse shoe – even down to the little marks which look like nails. However, there is also the tradition in the naming of plants to give animal names to what are thought to be inferior versions of finer things: dog rose, cow parsley, pignut, horse mushroom, horse radish, horse chestnut. The word horse is used to mean coarse and in the case of the supposedly inedible conker, it distinguishes it from the edible sweet chestnuts which, to this day, are roasted and sold on the pavement in London. The sweet chestnut tree, which is a native of Britain, is not related to the horse chestnut and the explanation for the name is convincing and appealing. The only problem with the coarse/horse explanation is that the tree is also known as a horse chestnut in Turkey. So maybe the name just spread with the tree and both were borrowed from the Turks. (see *Euro-conkers* page 55.)

Conkers of the world unite

The *aesculus* family of trees includes thirteen – or more – varieties growing in the northern temperate half of the world. All except one produce conkers – some in smooth and others in prickly shells – and vary considerably in height. They are found in the USA, Japan, India and China as well as Britain and there are various hybrids (cross-breeds). The red (flowered) horse chestnut, which is a cross between the horse chestnut and the American red buckeye, is common in England and may well be your local provider of conkers.

The name of the game

Dictionaries always call conkers a 'Boys' game' although girls go conkering and play conkers too – drawn, just like boys, by their beauty and their availability. There is little doubt that the word conker derives from conqueror – champion – and a game known as 'conquerors' existed long before the widespread planting of the horse chestnut tree. Anyway, the game of conkers as we know it has only been played for 145 years or so and the game of cob-nut was its true predecessor.

Cob-nut or cobs

The game was played using large hazel-nuts (also known as cob-nuts). The champion nut was known as the Cob Nut. A letter dated 1653 refers to objects being 'strung upon a ribban like the nutts boys play withall' and the game of cobs, cobblers, cock haw, conger or scabby was played in a similar way to conkers. Cob means both to strike and to outmatch. The game is recorded in Yorkshire, Leicestershire and Cheshire but also on the Isle of Wight and in Hampshire and Cornwall. Cobs was still being played in Yorkshire up to the second world war.

Conquerors

In the 18th century boys played a curious game with
striped snail shells called cogger, conquerors or even conkers. It was a messy business. The shells – sometimes still
attached to the poor old snail or 'pooty' as the poet John

Clare called it – were pressed against each other until one was smashed. The survivor was the Conqueror and a tally was kept. Clare kept his shells threaded on a string like a 'ribban' of cob-nuts and called the game cock fighting. It was also known as fighting cocks or cocks and hens and there is evidence that it was being played in Bristol in 1782. Conquerors was also played with stone marbles where one was thrown at another in the hope of splitting it. Once again the Conqueror's score was kept and two thousand years ago, the Roman poet Ovid described a similar game, only played with nuts. Conquerors was also played with walnut shells.

Conkers conquer the conquerors

When horse chestnuts displaced the snail shell and the cob-nut, the game continued to be called conquerors. But although the *new* game of conquerors also had its local names: cheggies, hongkongs, obbley-onkers, and even cobs, the term 'conkers' eventually replaced 'conquerors' nationwide. The first record of it being played with horse chestnuts is on the Isle of Wight in 1848 and the first mention in children's literature is in *Every Boy's Book*, 1856. One form of the game had the players sitting on a bench or log and facing each other. A piece of turf was laid flat between them and each player laid his conker in turn on the turf to be hit, instead of holding it up by its string. That apart, the ritual of the game was the same as the one we play today.

The great conker mystery

It was nearly 300 years after the horse chestnut tree was planted here that the first record of children playing conquerors with horse chestnuts occurred. No one has ever been able to resist picking up conkers so why did it take so long before children thought of playing conkers with them?

Early conker players needed protective clothing

No trees

The horse chestnut didn't spring from the ground fully formed and bearing conkers (it doesn't produce conkers until it is around twenty-five years old) and it was over a hundred years before it was widely distributed and established. From 1700 onwards, however, the craze for planting rows or avenues of trees quickened. The trouble was, they were on private estates and few children ever saw them.

Snails and cobs

Unlike horse chestnuts, hazel-nuts and snails could be found in every hedgerow and cottage garden patch and conquerors was largely a country game. Children used what was to hand. And when they did come across horse chestnut trees it probably never occurred to them to use them as conkers.

King Conker rules the estate

Between 1720 and 1820, roughly four million acres of common land which was free for everyone to use was 'enclosed' and turned into private park land. Children lost their natural playground and enclosure and the growth of industrial cities meant that thousands of people

moved to live in the cities. This great movement was accompanied by the arranging and altering of the landscape to suit the fashion of the time and the horse chestnut tree played an important part in the new fashion. In 1763, for example, the landscape gardener Capability Brown (1715-1783) planted 4800 horse chestnuts in the Tottenham Park estate in Wiltshire.

An early example of conkering?

In order to re-arrange the countryside to suit their own tastes, landowners were quite prepared to demolish an entire village if it spoiled their view. The Earl of Rochester was so outraged by schoolboys trespassing on his Dorset estate that in the 1770s he had the neighbouring village of Milton Abbas pulled down. The village was then re-built elsewhere – probably sited by Capability Brown – with each of the forty cottages sheltered by a horse chestnut tree. Maybe the schoolboys had pillaged his estate for conkers (see *Sticks and stones* page 45) and he thought that by planting conker trees in the street he'd discourage them. In the event, the trees were removed, because they made the cottages dark and damp.

Conkers take the waters

The spread of the horse chestnut tree, however, was not limited to huge estates. As the fashionable resorts where people went to 'take the waters' for their health began to expand, the tree was planted in their private squares and grander roads. The spa towns like Bath and Cheltenham – where I grew up and learned to play conkers – reached the peak of their fashionability in the Regency period (1811-1820) and the horse chestnut became an important townscape tree too.

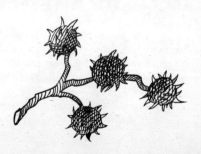

Conkers in the city

In the great industrial cities like Birmingham, Leeds, Sheffield and Manchester most children had nowhere to play together other than in the street. Then, after 1835, elected councils began to provide public parks. The fashionable horse chestnut was planted too and eventually the conker became familiar to the children of the town and the city rather than the countryside.

Conkers in the playground

While horse chestnut trees established themselves in every public park and recreation ground, the drive to ensure that every child had an education increased. In 1876 compulsory education up until the age of twelve was introduced and the conker entered the nation's playgrounds. Conkers became a game of the town and city and since then its popularity has never faltered. From the 1850s onwards, conquerors played with conkers ended the use of snail shells, walnut shells and cob-nuts, even in the country.

Conker cottages

In 1900, when the butterfly collector and famous naturalist Charles de Rothschild discovered an area which was the natural habitat of the rare Chequered Skipper butterfly, he bought the entire locality. He also had created on it a fashionably picturesque 'model' village which he gave to his bride as a wedding present. The village of Ashton, in Northamptonshire, is now the home of the World Conker Championships (see *In the beginning* page 85) and its stone-built and thatched cottages gather round the village green. Nearby is a horse chestnut avenue a mile long, which is the approach to the Rothschild mansion built at the same time. In 1900, too, a model 'village' of twenty houses was built round a green at Woodcote, Surrey and a fully grown horse chestnut was planted by the brand new smithy.

CHAPTER TWO

THE UNOFFICIAL HISTORY OF THE CONKER

Eve makes the first conker challenge

Noah took two conkers aboard the Ark

David conkers Goliath

William the Conkerer invades Britain

Conker picking in 1783

The first conker on the moon – 1969

CHAPTER THREE
THE CONKER

The fruit of the horse chestnut

That's what a conker is. The shell is the flesh and the conker is its seed. Just like a plum or a cherry – except they are tasty and sweet. It is the conker shell which protects it while it ripens and falls. In October the ground is littered with fallen leaves and conkers; by the first week of November the tree is bare. The seeds are dispersed by rats, rooks, squirrels, badgers and deer and so they are distributed and new conker trees take root. For most of us, there is no seed more instantly recognisable and none more beautiful than the conker.

Irresistible conkers

Who can resist picking up a conker? When you prise open its spiky shell you may find one or two or even three glossy brown seeds demanding to be taken home and ranged along your bedroom window ledge. If they fall from your pocket on the way home and you lose them you may even have done your bit in further distributing the tree. They only need an inch of soil cover and will take root in practically any conditions.

Cheesers or cheese cutters

Where two seeds occur in one shell they meet with flat faces but sometimes you'll find one of the potential cheese-cutters is further divided. Some conker players prefer cheese-cutters because they think they really do have the edge over round conkers. Three-in-a-bed conkers, though pretty, have no appeal for conker players. They are difficult to hit but are useless to hit with.

Conkering

In October conkers will fall naturally because they are ripe. The riper they are the more likely the shells are to split on impact and there is no need to bash them or jump on them to get the conkers out. Early fallers or conkers you've knocked down impatiently may well be unripe and still pure white inside their shells. The greenest spikiest shell is from the common horse chestnut but some less spiky or even smooth shells come from other varieties.

Conkering and conquering

When I was a child the conker season dominated the school playground for two or three weeks. We couldn't wait for the conkers to fall from the trees and went out with lumps of wood and chucked them into their lofty yellow summits. We filled carrier bags full of them and covered every window sill in the house. By the following day they had lost their shiny beauty so we gathered up our missiles and went out to down some more. We played conkers of course but, like many children, we enjoyed collecting them as much as anything. They were fruits we never ate but never grew tired of – the season was over before we got bored with them.

Sticks and stones

All conker collectors believe that the best ones grow at the top of the tree and heave lumps of wood and half-bricks up into its crown to bring them down. For some adult spoilsports this makes the horse chestnut a 'messy' tree because the leaves, split shells and debris which litter the ground are an offence to their eyes. There is no evidence that high conkers are better than low – just a feeling that those farthest from reach must be King Conkers, so the habit persists. As recently as September 1992 the *Daily Mirror* reported that a local councillor in Manchester wanted horse chestnut trees to be chemically neutered so that they wouldn't produce conkers – 'youngsters are risking their lives and damaging trees by climbing them'. Perhaps the tidy-minded councillor is unaware that a smaller, hybrid chestnut known as Baumann's horse chestnut produces double white flowers but no conkers. For this reason it is often planted in public places although a horse chestnut tree without chestnuts makes as much sense as a racehorse without a jockey.

More complaints

There have always been complaints about conkering. Over thirty years ago a vicar wrote to *The Times* complaining about the mess caused by trespassing children conkering in his vicarage grounds. And over forty years ago my cousin and I shied sticks, climbed trees and squeezed through fences to go conkering in other people's gardens. Once we were caught by a distant relative of that Manchester councillor. She threatened us with prison for stealing and made us cry. Even without falling out of trees we learned that conkering can be a pain as well as a pleasure. The outraged vicar, however, received little support from *Times* readers and the *Daily Mirror* left the last word on the proposed chemical neutering of horse chestnut trees to the reigning World Conker Champion, John Bull – 'This councillor wants neutering – he's round the twist.'

Keeping the shine

Nothing is more disappointing than finding that within a day of collecting them, the shine has gone off your hoard of conkers and in no time they are beginning to shrink. There is no way of preserving their natural shine although many children swear by keeping them in water.

It doesn't work. They look shiny while they're wet but they get dull just the same. Keeping them in the dark doesn't work either. If you want to plant them to grow a tree, do it as soon as possible. The older they are the less chance of taking root. Plant them while they're shiny.

What else can you do with conkers?

There are doll's house chairs made of conkers in the Museum of Childhood and in Bavaria, southern Germany, children cut faces in larger conkers like pumpkins on Halloween. Conker players make necklaces of conkers as a way of carrying them round but as adornment, conkers lose their charm as soon as they lose their shine.

Moth ball conkers

I once met an old lady collecting conkers – 'some for my grandson and some for me, we use them instead of moth balls' she told me, and a letter in the *Independent* in 1991 observed that it is a custom in Russia too.

Conker insurance

Even adverts on television show how much a part of our lives the conker has become. In 1992 an Equitable Life Assurance comercial showed a grandfather and grandson strolling down the chestnut avenue belonging to a stately home, and then playing conkers under the spreading chestnut tree. Grandad rambles on about how it was *his* father who'd planted the trees and how such wisdom had proved to be an investment for the future. Who would ever have imagined a century ago, that conkers would one day be used to sell insurance?

Conkers for colour and shine

Today, conkers are used in toiletries and Sainsbury's horse chestnut shampoo claims that, for brown hair, it will 'enhance the colour and shine'. It makes you wonder if those conkers the Turks fed to their horses also gave a bit of colour and shine to their coats. As for our own skin, Badedas and Bodyshop have both made shower gel with horse chestnuts but, so far, my skin has resolutely stayed the same colour. Maybe it's because conkers are also used as a sun-screening agent in anti-sunburn preparations.

Bitter conkers

In reference books conkers are usually described as the 'the fruit of the horse chestnut containing the inedible conker.' I suppose attempts have been made to eat the spiky shell but the conker looks more tempting and similar to the edible sweet chestnut. I have a dim recollection of nibbling a fragment from a shattered conker but the bitter taste discouraged me from knocking them back like Mars Bars. Anyway we are all brought up to believe that conkers are poisonous to humans. Nevertheless human beings will try to eat anything that is a berry, a fruit or a nut and, with rare exceptions, suffer nothing worse than a belly ache.

Poisonous conkers

The Ministry of Agriculture, Fisheries and Food had this to say in its publication *Poisonous plants and fungi* (HMSO 1988): 'Despite their bitter taste, children sometimes eat conkers, but seldom in sufficient quantities to cause severe poisoning; a mild stomach upset, with vomiting, is all that usually results. Eating large numbers, however, can be serious, leading to unconsciousness and even death; such incidents are extremely rare.' The poisonous substance is called aesculin, after the Latin name of the tree: 'It is present, particularly in the bark, flowers and young leaves, but the seeds (conkers) are also poisonous.'

Death by conkers

In *Poisonous plants in Britain and their effects on animals and men* (HMSO 1984) there is this account: 'A fatal case has been reported of a four year old boy who became restless then slept deeply after eating horse chestnuts. When, two days later, he ate a further quantity, he became unconscious and died in hospital from respiratory disease.' This poor boy's determination to eat bitter conkers regardless is unlikely to be repeated but if any of your friends get a belly ache and you know, or think, they've been eating conkers, get them to a doctor immediately.

The Dickens of a conker

Conkers are starch-based (as is bread) and Charles Dickens' magazine *Household Words* (December 1881) includes a method of making a 'strictly agreeable and edible flour' from conkers. It is very similar to that used by American Indians (see *Cowboys, Indians and buckeyes* page 102) and serves to reinforce the notion that the Victorians had a real thing about the horse chestnut – whether as an ornamental tree, a game of conkers or even as a food.

A Gypsy recipe

In his book *The Roots of Health*, Leon Petulengro also ignores the conkers-are-poisonous belief and insists that 'they are a great favourite of the Romanies either toasted over an open fire or boiled, then peeled and seasoned and sprinkled over sprouts or cabbage.' No mention of the bitter taste, but he warns that 'unless your teeth are very good so that they can grind the nuts small, or you take the trouble to grate or mince them, they can cause indigestion.'

Unpoisonous conkers?

On the continent and in America the horse chestnut doesn't seem to be regarded as poisonous. The famous French combined dictionary and encyclopedia published by Larousse describes the conker as 'edible' while the Spanish edition acknowledges its 'bitter taste' but does not describe it as inedible or poisonous.

Euro-conkers

In Turkey, the conker translates as horse chestnut which suggests that Europe not only adopted the tree, it also adopted its name. In Turkish 'at' is the word for horse, 'kestane' is the word for chestnut and the conker is an *atkestanesi* or an *at-kestanesi* or an *at kestanesi*. Choose your own conker.

French conkers

Larousse gives two definitions for horse chestnuts:
'*Une châtaigne*: Edible fruit of the horse chestnut tree, rich in starch.'
'*Une châtaigne* (slang): A smack in the gob.'
Larousse also credits the tree with a longer life than British sources and has a word for a chestnut grove.
'*Un châtaignier*: Jagged-leafed tree which can grow 35m in height and can survive several centuries. Its fruit, *les châtaignes*, are covered by a spiny husk.'

'*Une châtaigneraie*: a place planted with horse chestnuts.'
The French word for the shade of chestnut-coloured hair
we call brunette, is *châtain*.

Spanish conkers

Larousse gives this definition of a horse chestnut:
'*Un castaño de Indias* (literally: chestnut of India): Decora-
tive tree whose fruit resembles that of the sweet chestnut
but which has a bitter taste.'
'*Arrear una castaña*' (literally: urge on a chestnut) is slang
and means, again, a smack in the gob. '*Un castañazo*' is
slang for a punch.

A conk on the nose

It is strange how in France and Spain, where the game of
conkers is unknown, the horse chestnut is nonetheless
associated with hitting. To conk someone is to hit them

The conker

on the conk (nose) so conkers not only derives from con-querors (see *The name of the game* page 22) but also seems to have a separate connection with hitting – as in 'He conked him one'. Another slang use for conk, which I learned when I lived in North London, is to use it for head. (Conk is American slang for head too.) Nut as in 'Use your nut' also means head - hence 'He nutted him' – and the connection between nut, chestnut or conker, and hitting, is complete. And it's the same with the *châtaigne* and the *castañazo* in France and Spain.

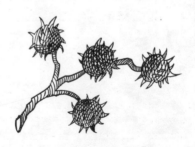

Conquers all known ills – well some of them

There's a deal of myth and mystery surrounding the conker but, in terms of its use as a 'natural' cure for common ills, there appears to be some substance in the claims that are made.

Are you sitting conkerfortably?

It's the height of the conker season and if you haven't got them ready-drilled and threaded on a string like beads, perhaps your pockets are stuffed with conkers. So what? Well, you are also guarding yourself against rheumatic pains and haemorrhoids or piles. A traditional country remedy, you see, is to keep a couple of conkers in your pocket at all times – replacing them only when they become as hard as a rock. Does it work? It appears to for believers, so you risk nothing by trying and there can be no harmful side effects. In fact, there are many patent medicines which use horse chestnuts as a basis for preparations used in the treatment of painful and enlarged veins and piles, as well as lumbago and muscular pains such as sprains and bruising.

Conkers get up your nose

Horse chestnut preparations are also used to treat inflammation of the nasal passages. The French seemed to know about this back in the reign (1715-1723) of Louis XV, when horse chestnut powder was classified as a kind of snuff used to increase natural secretions from the nose and provoke sneezing.

Conkers cool the blood

Even the bark of the horse chestnut was once used in the preparation of a medicine – known as a febrifuge – used to reduce fever. Folk medicine prescribed the use of the horse chestnut long before it was scientifically proven that conkers contain an ingredient which thins the blood and improves circulation.

Spike your tea with conkers

So, as an alternative to carrying conkers in your pocket, you can always make a tea from their dried and crushed spiky shells. A couple of cups a day gulped down between meals is good for all ills linked to poor circulation it is said and it makes a change from a tea bag. Dried and ground conkers have also been used as a coffee substitute.

Conkers wash whiter

Perhaps the horse chestnut's reputation as a natural cure has led to its use in shower gels. Certainly a traditional use was to soak and pulp them and use them for laundering and one of their ingredients, saponin (from which its poisonous ingredient stems) was made into soap. Internally and externally, conkers keep us clean it seems.

Kiwi conkers

In cricket, the new ball is often called a 'cherry' by the players – and commentators – because it is shiny and red. On 17th January 1992 I was listening to a test match commentary from New Zealand when I was startled to hear the Kiwi commentator refer to the new ball as a 'conker'. The horse chestnut tree is not indigenous to New Zealand but was apparently introduced there by British settlers. So, are conkers played in NZ? I asked the information officer at the New Zealand High Commission. No – he'd never seen or heard of conkers being played there but yes, he had heard of conkers. How was that? 'Well, we've all read about them in 'William' books which are very popular back home.'

The conker of Oz

So what about Australians – do they see a new cricket ball as a shining conker and do they play conkers with the same blue-chinned determination they play cricket? I went to Australia House: 'Conkers? Never heard of them. Oh you mean horse chestnuts. No probs. Got them in our parks in Melbourne for starters. The Brits brought them.'

Brits fail to conker India

The Indian horse chestnut (*aesculus indica*) is a native of the north west Himalayas. Despite the tree and despite the British presence in India I can find no account of conkers being played there. But I did find this account of Brits on a trip to the Himalayas in 1939: 'A profusion of magnificent fruits lay all around and it was quite impossible to leave them all there. We took a dozen or so each of the hardest and largest [conkers] for future contest. Ranikhet had a road along a ridge with wonderful vistas of the Himalayas to the north and towards the dusty plains on the south. In the bazaar there we solemnly played conkers. Nobody took the least notice. No crowd gathered; all were too busy or too polite to gape. We made up a few spares, gave them to some children and taught them how to play. "Do you think we have laid the foundations of the Kumaono-Tibetan conker championships?" asked Charlie.' Well if they did, the Ashton Conker Club (see *In the beginning* page 85) has yet to hear of it.

The Indian Conker Trick

CHAPTER FOUR
THE GAME

Tweedledum and Tweedledee agree to have a battle

A hisstory leson

Even the well-known 'skool spiv', Molesworth had
something to say about the history of conkers in *How to be
topp*

'Conkers is an old-fashioned game which hav been played
by generations of british boys. You kno what hapens you
pick up a huge horse chestnut which look absolutely super
like a derby winner and put some string through it. Then
you chalenge grabber or gilibrand who hav a conkerer of 20.
You say weedy things like

  Obbly obbly onker

  My first conker

  Hay ho hay nonny no ect.

Honour your oponent and turn round on the points of
your toes. After that you whirl your conker round and hurl
it at the dangling target hem-hem. Successful conkers are
always shriveled and weedy. Wot happens is that your
conker either shaters into a million pieces or flies through
the nearest window crash crash tinkle tinkle.' Molesworth's

spelling may be a bit off but his description of the game is dead on.

How to be topp by Willans and Searle

Who has first whack?

To decide who has first swipe, hitsy, donks or smack you have to gabble a little rhyme out faster than your opponent. In Cheltenham we used this rhyme:

> *Iddy iddy onker*
> *My first conker*
> *Iddy Iddy ack*
> *My first whack.*

But if I'd lived in Yorkshire I might have chanted:

> *Ally ally onker*
> *My first conker*
> *Quack quack*
> *My first smack*

Or you shout out: Bagsie firsie or First Donks or Firsy Jabs before your opponent and get the supposed advantage of the first hit.

Playing from memory

The traditional pattern of playing conkers has slight variations from one part of the country to the next, but one basic rule is standard throughout the country: players take alternate shots. The differences arise if your string gets 'twizzled' or plaited with your opponent's.

Hits and misses

If you hit your opponent's conker then he or she has a go at yours. If you miss you get two more tries for a hit and then it's your opponent's turn. If the strings tangle with each other, as a result of a miss, the first player to shout 'strings' gets an extra hit. In Cheltenham, I shouted

'tangles' to get an extra shot but elsewhere players shout their own local words like 'clinks', or 'clenches'. It is an underhand tactic to deliberately tangle and shout for an extra hit and a tangle can also, unfairly, force your opponent's conker down on to the string knot and so weaken it. Local rules may allow more than one shot for tangles and each time the strings tangle, your hand is chafed by the string.

Putting the boot in

Another local rule is 'stamps'. If your opponent drops his conker, or you knock it out of his hand, or if it is knocked off its string, you can shout 'stamps' and stamp on it, jump on it, or grind it with your heel. Having conquered it with your feet, this counts as a victory and you can add the defeated conker's score to your own conker's. But if your opponent manages to shout 'no stamps' first, then even if you crush it, you can't claim its score.

Heelies, wheelies, and ET

In Chris Powling's book *The Conker As Hard As A Diamond*, 'stamps' is known as 'heelies'. Another rule is 'wheelies', where you get an extra go if the conker you hit turns a complete circle on the end of its string. The book tells of the Conker Championship of the Universe in which the *Conker As Hard As A Diamond* competes with the American *Nuclear Rubber Bonker Conker*, the Russian *Hairy Octo-*

Conker and the ghostly shimmering *Conker From Outer Space*. Who wins? Ah – all I'll tell you is that the loser splits into 'umpteen million pieces each as light as a year.'

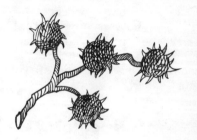

Conquered

Tradition demands that the game continues until the last little piece of conker clinging to the string is finally shattered and the string is bare. A conker may be broken by a blow from its rival but sometimes it breaks itself against it. Then the ritual of the score begins.

Scoring

A high score gives you playground cred and attitude. When you win a game you add one more to your tally plus the victories of your opponent's conker. If your conker is a three-er and your opponent's shattered conker was a five-er, yours now becomes a nine-er and so on. The conker which has beaten all the others in the street or playground or which is the winner of a conker championship is King Conker.

Specials

The ethics of doctoring your conker to improve its performance is a question of debate and custom (see *Fair play* page 91) which varies around the country. The least controversial method is to use an old conker because it is 'natural'. All you've got to do is to save some conkers from last season. These 'seasoners', or 'yearsies' will be shrunken, dull and harder than a 'straight' conker whether they've been put away in a dark cupboard or not. A conker two seasons old is called a 'second yearsie'.

High-tech

The methods of my childhood are primitive compared with the new techniques I've encountered – or heard of. The favoured method now is to put conkers in the micro-wave. Fans of this method claim it doesn't alter the conker's appearance. Others use the deep-freeze and swear that the conker doesn't even lose its shine. Coating with super-glue has its disciples too and I've read of one feind so determined to create a King Conker that he soaked it in vinegar, coated it with super-glue and then baked it in a potter's kiln. It sounds invincible, but must have looked like a glazed brown earthenware cupboard knob. Remember that super-glue is dangerous and should only be used with the help of an adult.

Low-tech

Baking and vinegar are the oldest known methods of hardening your potential Conqueror and are as old as the game. Older in fact because cob-nuts used to be hardened too. In the days when everybody had a fire in their hearth, conkers were left by the fire for a few days or shoved up the chimney. With care, they wouldn't look any different from 'seasoners'. The same applied to baking conkers in the oven. It had to be done in a low oven for about half an hour. The other method was to pickle them in vinegar but for how long they should be steeped was rarely discussed out loud. Some used brine (salt and water) or soda solution but if you wanted to pass your pickled conker off as a 'seasoner' you had to be careful the smell of vinegar didn't give it away.

The game

Gold conkers

Whether a 'straight' conker or a doctored one there is nothing within the accepted rules of the game to prevent you from decorating it. In 1992 a St Albans schoolboy carefully cut his conker in two and hollowed out the core. He then filled the cavity with Polyfilla and glued the halves together again with Araldite. Perhaps for decoration and perhaps to hide the join, he painted his all-conquering conker with gold paint. Despite its invincibility there was no shortage of challengers even though they must have realised that the Golden Conqueror was not quite as nature intended. Maybe it was like heavyweight boxing and everybody wanted a crack at the champion – no matter how the scales were tilted in his favour.

The most conquering conker

The Guinness Book of Records lists the most conquering conker as the one which won the BBC conker championship in 1954. It was a 'five thousander plus' according to the champion. A learned professor, however, has suggested that it might not have been a straight conker but an ivory – or Tagua – nut from the South American ivory palm which is a native tree of Colombia. *The Guinness Book of Records* now declares that it 'will not publish any category for the largest collection of conkers for fear that trees might suffer as a consequence.' So take the hint and don't damage trees when you go conkering (see *Green conkers* page 135).

CHAPTER FIVE

TIPS FOR WINNING

1 Use fully ripe, medium sized conkers. These will have fallen from the tree naturally and the spiky green shell will usually have split on impact with the ground. Remember: The larger the conker, the easier it is for your opponent to hit, but a small conker may fall apart when you make the hole.

2 Place a few spare conkers in a drawer for use next year as 'yearsies' and keep some conkers in a dry place for games with 'naturals'.

3 Either place your conkers on a baking tray and cook for 30 mins, Gas mark 4, 350°F (180°C) in a conventional oven or place in the microwave for 1 min. (You will find other ways of hardening your conker on pages 74-78).

or Place in a jam jar and cover with malt vinegar. Add one teaspoonful of sugar and leave overnight. Wash under running water and dry thoroughly with kitchen paper.

4 Check your conker for hairline cracks. Only use conkers which have survived the hardening process intact.

5 Place your conker on a board with the pale patch uppermost and make a hole with a skewer. The hole should be only slightly bigger than the lace.

6 Thread your conker on to a leather lace measuring about 53cms. Leather is better than string as it won't cut into the conker.

7 You will probably devise your own technique for hitting, depending on whether you are left or right handed, but the most important thing is to concentrate hard on your opponent's conker. Wait until it is completely still, aim at the top of the conker, pull your conker towards you so that the string is tight, then swing your conker hard for a clean strike. Each player takes it in turn to strike, and the game ends when one of the conkers is completely removed from the lace.

Note: Before you begin your conker match, decide with your opponent whether you are going to play with 'specials' (those which have been hardened), 'yearsies' (conkers saved from the previous year) or 'naturals'. Conkers is a game of trust and before you begin, each player must declare truthfully the number of previous wins with that conker. The winner then adds that number to the score of the winning conker.

CHAPTER SIX

THE WORLD CONKER CHAMPIONSHIPS

Donks in Derbyshire

There have always been playground conker contests but in 1960 a local grocer, George Gibson, decided to put his village, Walton-on-Trent, on the sporting map. The 700 year old village planned to hold the contest under the spreading chestnut trees on the banks of the Trent but, come the great day, it rained. Of course. Nothing daunted, the contest was shifted to the village street and many of the 500 villagers turned up despite the downpour. There were three age classes and a final to determine the King Conker. Of the twenty-eight boys who competed, the youngest was six and the oldest, Michael Clarke, was thirteen. Dennis Hall, aged eight, soaked his conker overnight in vinegar and went on to win the 8-10 class, but he was beaten in the King Conker final by Michael Clarke who had put his faith in baking. In 1961, ten year old Michael Howells, using a four year old conker, became King Conqueror and by 1969 the contest was listed as an annual event in a book about English customs and traditions. Unfortunately the tradition soon died out. Moral: It takes more than a keen grocer to weigh up a load of old conkers.

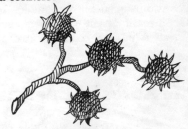

In the beginning

It was in Ashton, Northamptonshire, in 1965, that the first World Conker Championship took place and the Ashton Conker Club has promoted and organised it ever since. It all began when a group of locals were sitting in Ashton's pub, The Three Horse Shoes. They were fed up because the weather was too bad for a fishing trip. They decided to hold a conker championship instead. It was agreed to play for a cup – I've seen the first winner's inscription and the cup says 'World Champion' – and because one of the contestants had a blind relative, a whip-round was made for charity. And from such little conkers, hoary old chest-nuts grow. Since then Ashton has been blessed with good weather – only two bad Sundays in 28 championships.

The Rules of Engagement

1. The contest is to take place on the Green at Ashton on the second Sunday in October.
2. All conkers and strings are to be supplied by the Ashton Conker Club.
3. Each competitor is to take three alternate strikes until one of the conkers is shattered.
4. The contestant with a conker intact is declared the winner, but if either or both conkers are dislodged by a snag the game is declared void and restarted.
5. Three snags will lead to the disqualification of a contestant.

6. The length of lace in play must be no less than eight inches a strike.

7. There will be three stewards in charge of each section and their decision will be final.

8. If a game lasts more than five minutes the stewards may, at their discretion, award the game to the contestant with the highest number of successful strikes made after each has had nine more attempts.

Title and distinction

The World Conker Championships now have four titles: Men, Women, Junior (under 15) and Team. Until 1986 there was only one Champion of the World and then additional categories were introduced. A feature of the championships is that there is no King Conker. The contestants draw a new conker for each round and so the finals are played with untried conkers. Of course they are all 'straight'. I am a believer that a good conker will always beat a poor one, but the fact that five of the past world champions have won the title more than once leads many to believe that technique is all.

Technique or luck?

Some players prefer to hit down on the conker to force it against the knot in the 'string', while others attack from the side. Once the skin of the conker has been split a player will attack it like a boxer aiming at his opponent's cut eye. Some like round conkers, others prefer a slightly oval shape – not that there's much variation at Ashton, where conkers are selected for even size and shape. It's all in the luck of the draw whether you get a hard or soft conker or a sound conker or one with a hidden flaw. The late Ron Marsh, a founder member of the Ashton Conker Club, was a legendary Conqueror. He was the first ever World Champion and won it again in 1972. Ron was also a losing finalist so maybe he knew something about technique *and* luck.

In it for the money

Not only are the traditions of conkers observed at Ashton but, since that first impromptu championship, the tradition of supporting charities for the blind has continued. So far, through entry fees, sponsorship of individual players and commercial sponsorship of the event itself, programme advertising, competitions and contributions from the range of sideshows and stalls which the championships attract, the Ashton Conker Club has donated over £80,000 to charities for the blind.

Conkers pull in the crowds

Games of conkers at school can draw a crowd in a playground but compared with the World Championships they are strictly minor league. Ashton now attracts crowds of over 4000. Even in 1992, when the awful weather reduced the attendance, the championships still raised £10,000, of which £5000 went to the Royal National Institute for the Blind (for talking books) and the remainder went to local charities for the visually handicapped. In the 1992 championships a player with a guide dog and a sighted 'second' progressed to the third round. The 'second' helped to line up the shot and more often than not, the sightless player did the business and got in a good whack.

Fair play

When I was a boy and playing conkers in Gloucestershire, players suspected of tampering with their conkers were regarded as cheats. Even carefully hoarded yearsies were a bit suspect but baking or steeping in vinegar was regarded with the same distaste as is doping (drug use) in athletics. Some boys were suspected of coating their conkers with model aeroplane maker's 'dope' to give a yearsie a 'straight' conker's shine. There's no cheating at Ashton.

Cheating

In the aftermath of the great test match ball-tampering controversy of the summer of 1992 the following note appeared in the World Conker Championships programme: 'Cheating – this very rare occurence has never been proved, but it has been hinted that one or two players have been seen scuffing one side of the conker to effect an unnatural swing (a cobbling). This would unnerve the opponent who would not know on which side his conker was going to be struck. Stewards have been alerted and a keen eye will be kept open for this practice.'

Naturals

There is no shortage of conkers around Ashton village but an entry of around 400 players creates a great demand. In all about 2000 conkers need to be collected (straight from the tree) but with a chestnut avenue on the Rothschild estate nearby, quantity is not a problem. They have to be selected for even size though and it is a huge task to bore them all and thread them on to leather boot laces. The Hon. Miriam (Rothschild) Lane CBE – the author and naturalist who owns the estate – provides the conkers. The laces come from nearby Northampton which, conveniently, is the centre of the shoe-making industry. At the championships you draw your conker from a cloth bag with only the laces showing. There's no chance of tampering with the championship conkers, even if you are devious enough to want to. Mrs Lane allowed the Ashton Conker Club to plant twenty-five horse chestnut saplings around the village to celebrate the championships' silver jubilee.

Conker headquarters

The headquarters of the Ashton Conker Club is a stone and thatch pub on the Ashton village green. The green is ringed with conker trees and the Three Horse Shoes pub was doubtless a reference to that old chestnut about blacksmiths and spreading chestnut trees. In 1971 the pub was re-named *The Chequered Skipper* after the rare – now locally extinct – butterfly which attracted Charles de Rothschild to the estate in the first place. Despite the name change the pub is still the hub around which the championships revolve. A local folk group called Empty Pocket always performs in the pub on championship Sunday and one of the musicians, Mike Milne, wrote this song specially for the event.

Conkers

Under the spreading chestnut tree,
The village blacksmith sings:
Amusing himself,
Confusing himself,
And threading his nuts on a string!

Chorus: *Conkers! Conkers!*
Proud fruit of the chestnut tree:
True love conquers everything
And I shall conquer thee.

1.   *For more'n twenty years, in the village of Ashton,*
In the Northants countryside,
They got themselves a bit of competition,
To salvage National Pride.
In October, on the green, a'fore the Chequered Skipper,
There's many that make the trip,
To take their chance with their arm and the weather,
In the Conker Championship.

2.   *Now there's some that try to boil 'em and others try to*
        bake 'em,
     Or cover them with cement:
     But the best sort of conker's the one that's a natural,
     That's swung with good intent.
     The secret's in the action and the movement of the
        elbow,
     As you let your chestnut fly;
     You stare 'em in the eye 'til they's all disconcerted,
     And unleash that awful cry:

3.   *Many years ago, a chap called William,*
     Came over the sea from France;
     On his way to Ashton, with his second called Norman,
     He really fancied his chance.
     But King Harold took exception to this foreign
        intervention,
     And put an army in his way:
     But he got one in the eye and that's why William's
     Called 'Conqueror' to this day!

The World Conker Championships

Chorus: *Conkers! Conkers!*
          Proud fruit of the chestnut tree;
          True love conquers everything
          And I shall conquer thee!

© Mike Milne/Empty Pocket 1988

Conquerors cross continents

Although there is no evidence of conkers being played anywhere else in the world, Ashton Conker Club's claim that theirs is a world championship is not an empty boast. Over the years players have come from Australia, Canada, Denmark, France, Germany, Holland, Japan, Malta, Mexico, New Zealand, USSR (then) and USA. A Dutch player once cycled all the way to compete and the Mexican player, R. Ramirez, was World Champion in 1976 – the only time the title has left the country.

Conker war aids world peace

As the Cold War thawed at the end of the 1980s, the London correspondent of the Soviet news agency TASS played and beat an American in the first round of the championships. The American was a regular competitor and flew in specially for the event.

CHAPTER SEVEN

AMERICAN CONKERS

Buckeyes

If the British are bonkers about conkers, then the Americans – well the Ohioans – are crazy about buckeyes. Ohioans are even called 'buckeyes' and on car and truck licence plates in Ohio the words 'The Buckeye State' are printed below the number. The official tree of the state is the buckeye tree and the traditional Ohio Buckeye Candy is made in the shape of buckeyes. It is popular for picnicking, parties and other festive occasions.

Conker candy

This is the recipe from America, where they call it Buckeye Candy. You will need:

225g (8oz) smooth peanut butter
275g (10oz) icing sugar
25g (2oz) soft margarine or softened butter
225g (8oz) cooking chocolate
cocktail sticks

American Conkers

These quantities will make about twenty-five conk‌

Melt the chocolate in a bowl over a saucepan of water. While the chocolate is melting, mix together thoroughly the peanut butter, sifted icing sugar and margarine. If the mixture is too sticky add some more icing sugar. When the mixture is stiff, roll it into balls the size of conkers. Using a cocktail stick, dip each ball into the melted chocolate until it is almost covered leaving some of the peanut butter mixture exposed on top. Place each conker on a plate covered with greaseproof paper and place in the refrigerator for two hours to harden. Enjoy!

American cousins

Just as the horse chestnut is the name we give to both our tree and its seed, so too is buckeye the name of the tree and its seed. In fact the term conker and the game is unknown in the USA so it is the Ohio buckeye, not the horse chestnut, which is the state's official tree. Both belong to the same chestnut tree family but the native Ohio buckeye is much smaller than the horse chestnut. Although its seeds are a similar size to horse chestnuts the tree grows not much more than 9m high. Its flower is greeny-yellow and its buckeye case is brown and smoother than our conker's green spikes. Its botanical name is *aesculus glabra*, which derives from glabrous – meaning smooth-skinned – and the tree is found in central and south east USA.

Cowboys, Indians and buckeyes

It was the Indians of Ohio who gave the native chestnut tree its name. The brown chestnuts, with their pale oval pupils, looked like the eye of a male deer or buck so they called them 'buck-eyes'. The European ranchers adopted the name and the Indians, inadvertently, christened their own lost land 'The Buckeye State'. Western American Indians used the 'Californian horse chestnut' to make 'gruel or soup', while 'Californian Indians pulverize the nut, extract the bitterness by washing with water and form the residue into a cake to be used as food.'

Buckeye barmy

A full-colour 32-page catalogue is published by the Ohio University Students' Association in which everything – but *everything* – is printed, stamped, incised, transferred, sewn, etched, painted, enamelled or carved, with buck-eyes or conkers. Nothing is too small – a golf ball marker – or insignificant – a paper napkin – or bizarre – a windsock for your private aeroplane – to avoid the buckeye logo. There's a whole range of baby clothing including potty-training pants which are worn over a nappy and have the slogan 'Buckeye in training' printed on the bottom. You can even get a 'real buckeye hand-dipped in 24-carat gold overlay with a 24" gold tone chain'.

Conkers in Columbus?

Ohio State Univesity is the biggest in the USA with 58,000 full-time students. Sport is a big thing at Ohio State and it has its own huge horse-shoe shaped stadium. Appropriately there is a stand of 82 horse chestnuts – buckeyes rather – nearby which started out with the ten planted to honour the university's champion grid-iron football team of 1930. Strangely there aren't that many buckeyes on the campus or in the city. If conkers ever caught on in the university there might be a shortage of buckeyes to play with. But without a tradition of conker playing, it would be hard for the game to take root. It is, after all, a game for children and the circumstances which led to it becoming one of our great games of street and playground do not apply in Ohio. Maybe it could take off as a campus game for adults – well students – but perhaps they love their Ohio buckeyes too much to want to batter them to pieces.

CHAPTER EIGHT

HORSE CHESTNUTS AND CHESTNUT HORSES

A horse of a different colour

Everybody knows that 'chestnut' also means a reddish-brown colour. The colour of a conker in fact. But sweet chestnuts are brown too, so does the chestnut horse take its name from the horse chestnut or the sweet chestnut? And what is a chestnut horse anyway. In *As You Like It* Shakespeare says 'Your chestnut hair was ever the only colour' and a horse was first attested as 'chestnut-coloured' in 1636. *As You Like It* was written around 1600 so both references occur long after the horse chestnut tree was established in England. But quite apart from the colour there are other, and confusing, links between horse and conker.

Red horses

'Chestnut' is a common colour in horses and describes a range of colour from a pale golden brown to a very dark red-brown. The darkest horses are known as liver-chest-

Horse chestnuts and chestnut horses

A chestnut was mentioned by Shakespeare

nuts. A *true* chestnut has a chestnut mane and tail. These may be darker or lighter than the body colour tone but *lesser* chestnuts have flaxen or golden manes and tails. Chestnuts are sometimes thought to be 'flashy' or unreliable – particularly if they have white on their feet.

A chestnut winning the Derby

Flashy tree – flashy horse

Admirers of native English trees like oak, ash, elm and beech sometimes dismiss the imported and merely ornamental horse chestnut as 'flashy' and it is an interesting coincidence that the same word is used for the chestnut horse. The racehorse, The Minstrel, who won both the Derby and the Irish Derby in 1977, was a chestnut with a white blaze and four white socks – more than enough to damn him in the eyes of those who swear by this rhyme:

> *One white foot, ride him for your life.*
> *Two white feet, give him to your wife.*
> *Three white feet, give him to your man.*
> *Four white feet, sell him – if you can!*

I bet you've all prised open a shell too early in the conker season and found an unripe conker with patches of white on its glossy chestnut brilliance.

Chestnuts in season

It is claimed that all Thoroughbred racehorses have an ancestry which can be traced back to a chestnut racehorse who was foaled in 1764. Eclipse is usually acknowledged as the greatest racehorse ever and his skeleton, which was once in the Natural History Museum, now has a place of honour at the National Horse Racing Museum at Newmarket. Among his famous chestnut descendants are the Derby winners, Shahrastani (1988), Nashwan (1989), Generous (1991) and the Grand National winners, Mr Frisk (1990) and Seagram (1991).

But are chestnuts good for horses?

In his book about folk medicine the French author Jean Palaiseul gives a horse chestnut recipe for a mash for feeding to horses. The conkers are reduced to flour, mixed with oats and administered in the amount of 100 grammes per day as medicine for broken-winded horses: 'a purpose for which it is still used by the Turks and to which it owes both its scientific and common name.' Another source (*Poisonous plants and fungi*, HMSO 1988) states that conker leaves are browsed by animals without apparent ill effect but that, 'poisoning, most probably by the conkers, has been reported in cattle, horses and pigs'. Yet another (*Poisonous plants in Britain and their effects on animals and men*, HMSO 1984) reports that, 'the young leaves of the tree are usually considered the most toxic . . . but horse chestnuts rarely cause problems [to animals] in Britain.' Horse chestnut bark is considered to be poisonous too but cattle and horses are known to gnaw it sometimes and an extract from the bark is used in veterinary medicine. Probably the greatest value the conker tree has to horses is to provide shade and to be a good itching post.

Horse hides and racing silks

It is via the bark of the tree that, perhaps, the most curious link between chestnut horses and horse chestnuts occurs. The bark contains a substance used in tanning animal hides and for dying silk and cotton black. It is quite possible that a jockey riding a chestnut racehorse is seated on a leather saddle, shod in leather boots and dressed in racing silks, all of whose manufacture owes something to horse chestnut bark.

Chestnuts on a chestnut

On the legs of all horses there is a little knob of hard skin called a 'chestnut' – perhaps the last vestige of a toe. The Oxford dictionary entry of 1859 included an odd method to tame a horse: 'using the chestnut of his leg, which they dry, grind . . . and blow into his nostrils.'

Mr President conquers slavery

The sixteenth president of the USA, Abraham Lincoln, is remembered for two things: he ended black slavery in America and he was assassinated. In 1858 he accused an opponent of using: 'a specious and fantastic arrangement of words by which a man can prove a horse chestnut to be a chestnut horse.'

CHAPTER NINE

CHESTNUT AVENUE AND CHESTNUT SUNDAY

A conker duel in 1841

A riddle

What do the architect who designed St Paul's Cathedral, a diarist, Queen Victoria, a Radio One disc jockey and our present Queen have in common? Answer: conkers. Well, more exactly, they all have a connection with Chestnut

Avenue in Bushy Park and the growth in popularity of the horse chestnut tree throughout Britain. Bushy Park, you see, is a thousand acre deer park attached to the royal palace of Hampton Court and during the reign of William III and Mary of Orange (Holland) it was a flat uninteresting area of hawthorn and scrub. Or so thought the King and he decided to take it in hand.

The architect

Hampton Court was the second most important royal palace – St James's in Pall Mall was the first – but the King was determined to make it his home and extend it with a new wing. The great architect, Sir Christopher Wren, was employed to design the extension and the improvements to the grounds.

The diarist

In 1664 the diarist, author and botanist, John Evelyn, published his book *Sylva* (it means wood) and noted that chestnut avenues were 'all the rage' in France – the Luxembourg Gardens and the Champs Elysées in Paris for example - and Wren seized on the idea of laying out a grand avenue of horse chestnuts which would convey the King in triumph to the new wing of his palace. Construction began in 1699 immediately after William and Mary departed on their annual June visit to Holland and by the end of the year the entire avenue had been laid out and planted.

Conkers to the east and conkers to the west

Chestnut Avenue runs north to south and ends with a grand circle where it divides around a statue sited in the middle of an ornamental pond. Including the circle the avenue is exactly one mile long. It is lined on each side with 137 horse chestnuts.

Whirlwinds and storms

In 1703 a 'whirlwind' did enormous damage to the four year old trees but they were easily replaced. In 1908 it was a different story. A great storm levelled seventy limes and twelve chestnuts in one minute. All of them were perfectly sound – many of them over 30m high – and the carnage attracted thousands of sight-seers including Edward VII. In 1909 new trees were planted to replace those destroyed.

Hurricanes too

The two great 'hurricanes' of our times – one in 1987 and another in 1989 - deprived many boys and girls of their favourite conker trees and damage caused to woodland across the British Isles was treated as a national disaster. Fortunately damage to Chestnut Avenue was less extensive than expected. Only ten chestnuts were destroyed – it's estimated that 15 million trees were destroyed on the night of 16/17 October 1987 – and these would probably have been the older trees. The life span of horse chestnuts is considerable and the oldest dated trees in Britain were planted in 1664.

Queen conker

William III died in 1702 and never saw the avenue in maturity and royal interest in it fluctuated down the years. In February 1989, however, Queen Elizabeth II planted a horse chestnut sapling to replace one of the hurricane victims.

Conkers by appointment

In 1837 the re-built Buckingham Palace became the principal London home of the Royal Family and in 1838 Queen Victoria opened Hampton Court to the public. The consequences were sensational. The chestnut trees were now

140 years old and at their most magnificent. To the ordinary Londoner, Bushy Park was a wonderful new playground and Chestnut Avenue a glorious revelation. As its fame grew, more and more visitors flocked to it and from mid-century until the outbreak of the first world war in 1914, it was one of the sights of London. In October the avenue must have rained conkers and it still does. Coincidentally, it was in the 1850s that children began to use conkers instead of snail shells when playing the game that was still known, then, as conquerors.

The American squirrels arrive

As the popularity of the game of conkers grew during the nineteenth century, children collecting conkers in Chestnut Avenue would have had to compete with the deer – there is still a herd of over 300 in Bushy Park – and the squirrels. For the park played another part in botanical history. In 1890, five American squirrels from New Jersey were introduced – reputedly the first grey squirrels in

England. They – like the deer – will eat the beautiful seeds of the horse chestnut tree. Maybe that was why they were introduced into Bushy Park in the first place.

Chestnut Sunday

Chestnut Avenue attracted crowds on any public holiday but in May it was at its best. The mile of green cliffs hung with tapered white candles of blossom and with the deer browsing in their shade, it was a scene unequalled in Britain and, probably, Europe. And, somehow, the nearest Sunday to the 11th of May became known as Chestnut Sunday. From the 1880s, the *Times* newspaper noted, 'Buses, taverns, hotels and teashops combined to advertise 'Chestnut Sunday' – the day when the bloom of the trees is considered to be at its best.'

Chestnut Sunday becomes a golden oldie

After the first world war Chestnut Sunday declined and the tradition had ended by the outbreak of the second world war. In 1970 the Radio One disc jockey, Mike Raven, tried to revive it but the glory days were over. People will always admire the splendour of Wren's Chestnut Avenue in its May blossom, however, and boys and girls will always go conkering there in October.

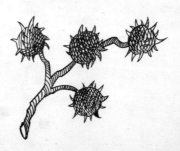

CHAPTER TEN

TEN THINGS YOU DIDN'T KNOW ABOUT CONKERS

There was an old man from Yonkers,
Who was mortally afraid of conkers,
He sat on a rail, with his head in a pail,
And went slowly and noisily bonkers.

1. Blue conkers

Here's a trick. Snap off a twig from a conker tree and scrape some of the bark into a glass of water. Let the bark soak – but not so long it turns the water yellow – then hold the glass up to the sun or shine your bike lamp through it. There should appear in the water a lovely luminous sky-blue colour or fluorescence. Strangely, the bark from the South American cinchona tree will also give a blue fluorescence. The drug quinine is extracted from the bark of the cinchona and a febrifuge (see *Conkers cool the blood* page 61) prepared from the bark of horse chestnut branches was used in France as an alternative to quinine.

2. Exploding conkers

Sometimes a clean hit by a King Conker can cause the victim to shatter into fragments as though it had exploded. Not so very surprising, therefore, that conkers should have been used in the manufacture of explosives. During the first world war of 1914-1918, Britain used a substance called acetone to make explosives. But acetone was in short supply, so Chaim Weizmann, a scientist working at Manchester University, discovered a method of making acetone from the starch in maize (Indian corn). As the war progressed German submarines stopped the ships from bringing corn into the country so an alternative had to be found. Chaim Weizmann turned to the conker, as it too contains starch. The process worked and nationwide conker collections were made, mainly by children, and the acetone shortage was overcome. Conker collections were organised again during the second world war of 1939-1945 so Chaim Weizmann played an important part in the overthrow of Hitler. When, in 1948, the Jewish state of Israel was founded, he became its first President.

3. Goal keepers conkered

The shaven-nutted, sharp-elbowed and boney-kneed Wolverhampton Wanderers and England centre-forward, Steve Bull, is known to his fans as 'Bully'. In a spoof profile his favourite food is listed as 'conkers in gravy'. In England, the first victory of your conker makes it a 'one-er'. In Scotland a one-er is known as a 'bull' or a 'bully-one'. So far as scoring goals for Wolverhampton Wanderers is concerned, 'Bully' must be around a hundred-er. Could be something to do with his diet.

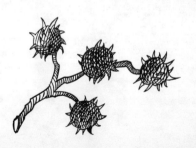

4. Putting chestnuts on the map

In the London A-Z street guide there are fifty-six 'Chestnut' entries. There are fifteen 'Chestnut Avenues' alone, including Wren's avenue at Hampton Court (see *Chestnut Sunday* page 122) and after the oak, ash and elm entries the 'Chestnut' list is the most numerous. Nothing indicates more obviously the impact that the horse chestnut tree has had on our lives. There is also a Chestnut Grove and a Chesnut Road. 'Chesnut' is the old spelling of 'Chestnut'. Wherever you live I bet you've got a Chestnut Avenue, Grove, Street or Road somewhere near you.

5. Nutty about the 'Chestnut Tree'

At the end of the 1930s the dance halls of Britain were gripped by a curious dance-game-song craze called: 'Underneath the Spreading Chestnut Tree'. Soon after it was written, photographs appeared in the papers of King George VI performing it at a Boy Scout Jamboree. Like the 'Okey Kokey' and 'The Conga' it became all the rage. Years later it was even recorded by Pinky and Perky. Your grandparents will show you how to do it but it's dead easy: on the word 'spreading' you spread your arms, on the word 'chest', you put your hands on your chest, on the word 'nut' you put your hands on your head and on the word 'tree' you raise your arms like branches. The song and dance craze may be over, but the conker craze comes back every year.

6. Horse chestnut records (1)

The tallest recorded tree was measured at Ashford Chase in Hampshire in 1984 when it was 39m high. (*Guinness Book of Records 1993.*)

The greatest girth was recorded at Andover, Hampshire in 1983 when the tree measured 6.7m round its trunk.

A tree is recorded at Hawkshurst, Kent as 'covering an area of 285 ft in circumference'. That means a total spread of approximately 28m but there are probably greater spreads in existence.

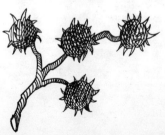

7. Horse chestnut records (2)

There was a record called (and spelled) 'Conkers' by one Mike Terry on Joy Records (Joys 233) released in November 1972. 'Chestnut Tree' (see *Nutty about the 'Chestnut Tree'* page 132) was also recorded by the Massed Bands of Aldershot and Eastern Command.

8.   Green conkers

One morning in 1991, just before dawn in the French town of Strasbourg, a whole avenue of horse chestnut trees was cut down to make way for a new tramway system. The trees were over a hundred years old. The felling led to a pitched battle between defenders of the environment and riot police with tear gas.

9. Conker clones

There have been several attempts to replace the beautiful natural conker with a man-made one. In the 1960s there appeared a game with plastic conkers. When the conkers were broken they could be reassembled with interlocking pieces. A similar toy was sold in street markets in the 1970s. This time the conkers were made from red and yellow striped plastic and were possibly made in Taiwan or Korea.

10. The Konka fails to conquer

On the 25th September 1953, the *Eagle* comic carried the following advertisement:

'A strike on his conk and off flies his cap. They're smashers. Eagle Konka price 2/11. The new game. Fits every schoolboy's pocket. Enter the National Eagle Konka Championship and Win a Super Bike for Christmas.'

For 2/11 (15p now) you could go to the cinema or a football match. The Konka didn't catch on; it was a doomed venture. Natural conkers are free and you've only got to pick them up to have a game. They come and go before you have a chance to get tired of them and everybody knows how to play.

Conkers are part of the seasonal order of our lives and you will never quite grow out of the fun of shattering your opponent's conker into a million pieces.

WE ARE THE CHAMPIONS

World Conker Champions

Men

1965	R. W. Marsh	1977	G. Childs
1966	S. J. Walden	1978	L. Treliving
1967	L. Collins	1979	C. Bray
1968	T. Winham	1980	K. Height
1969	P. Midlane	1981	W. Cox
1970	J. M. Hillyard	1982	J. Blackman
1971	T. Dix	1983	S. Rowan
1972	R. Marsh	1984	R. Langer
1973	P. Midlane	1985	P. Midlane
1974	J. Marsh	1986	C. Bray
1975	J. Marsh	1987	J. Hawes
1976	R. Ramirez	1988	W. Cox

| 1989 | P. Shortt | 1991 | J. Bull |
| 1990 | H. Watson | 1992 | P. Canning |

Women

1988	S. Doubleday	1991	P. Baker
1989	C. Bateman	1992	J. Courtney
1990	M. Bedford		

Junior

1986	C. Bilson (10–15 yrs)	1990	F. Elliott
	L. Bilson (5–9 yrs)	1991	L. Crewe
1987	M. Nikel	1992	M. Hutcheson
1989	F. Kingdom (Girls)		
	P. Lempriere (Boys)		

If you would like to take part in the World Conker Championship please contact the Ashton Conker Club Headquarters, The Chequered Skipper, Ashton, Oundle, Northants. Tel: 0832 273494.